THE
LITTLE BOOK
OF

PRIDE
HEROES

ICONS OF
THE LGBTQIA+
COMMUNITY

THE
LITTLE BOOK
OF

PRIDE
HEROES

ICONS OF THE LGBTQIA+ COMMUNITY

JARED
RICHARDS

♥

ILLUSTRATED BY
PHIL CONSTANTINESCO

Smith
Street
Books

CONTENTS

INTRODUCTION

Long before the 1969 Stonewall Riots ignited the modern gay rights movement, LGBTQIA+ people have found strength in community and each other. Thankfully, we live in a time where there's no shortage of queer heroes to look to for inspiration – just the beginning of the rainbow, this book spotlights 52 LGBTQIA+ trailblazers across 50 entries, while touching upon lots more along the way.

From activists to artists, politicians to code-breaking mathematicians, these queer icons aren't altruistic, untouchable figures. They are, like you or me, humans – messy and complicated people who have often led hard lives and battled internal demons, compounded by discrimination and hatred. But even among the darkness, these pages glow with their light, love and joy, as these people helped to open closed minds and change the world by being themselves.

Identity is complex, deeply personal and, for many, ever-shifting – the language queer people use to express their sexuality and gender, including a refusal to label themselves at all, should be respected. We've taken cues from each icon on their pronouns and identity (as at time of printing), and resisted the urge to label the unlabelled, or use terms that weren't common use during their day.

While we've come so far, the fight for LGBTQIA+ equality is far from over and Pride continues to be of utmost importance. Currently, same-sex relations are illegal in 65 countries; queer people face violence across the globe, and anti-LGBTQIA+ legislation is on the rise in so-called "progressive" countries like the US and UK, targeting trans and gender-diverse people. Whether you're part of our community or an ally, I hope these stories inspire you to live truthfully and continue pushing for LGBTQIA+ liberation everywhere.

MARSHA P JOHNSON

1945–1992, United States

Whether or not Marsha P Johnson instigated the 1969 Stonewall Riots as some accounts claim, her activism and legacy as a trailblazer for queer rights go far beyond that pivotal day.

Born in New Jersey, Marsha moved to Manhattan's bohemian Greenwich Village in the 1960s, finding herself as a drag queen, self-identified transvestite (while she's often referred to as a trans woman, the term was not commonly used at the time) and community leader. Often spotted wearing a flower crown, Johnson's generosity and spirit in the face of her own hardships and poverty saw her referred to as "Saint Marsha" across the Village.

While some historians place her at the heart of the Stonewall Riots, Marsha herself claimed to have joined the protests later. Regardless, she soon grew frustrated by the movement's focus on white gay males, and, with activist Sylvia Rivera (see page 26), co-founded STAR, one of the first transgender and homeless youth housing organisations. While short-lived – funded primarily by Rivera's and Johnson's sex work – its impact was monumental. Before her death in 1992, widely believed by the community to be a murder but treated by police at the time as a suicide, Marsha constantly fought for the LGBTQIA+ community to respect all within it.

AND ONE MORE THING ...

Johnson said her middle initial stood for "Pay it no mind!"

GILBERT AND GEORGE

Born 1943, Italy & 1942, England

The only "Living Sculpture" you'll find in this book, art duo and husbands Gilbert Prousch and George Passmore prefer to think of themselves as a single artistic unit – one sculpture, not two. You'll almost never see Gilbert without George, and you're even less likely to catch either dressed in anything but a tweed suit. Since finding each other in 1967 while studying sculpture in London, they've been inseparable, shaping British contemporary art in the process.

Ever provocative, their profanity-laden and occasionally obscene work – a multimedia grab-bag of performance, photography, charcoal drawings and more – is inspired by the sights of their long-time stomping ground East London, from street signs to skinheads.

Under the motto "art for all", they aim to eradicate the distinction between stuffy galleries and everyday life, not only by capturing the world around them in their work but by being art themselves. Perhaps their most controversial output has been their own conservative politics and repeated adoration of Margaret Thatcher – a bold position as queer people and artists alike. Avoiding easy categorisation even in their eighties, the two continue to provoke and challenge what art and artists should be.

AND ONE MORE THING ...
In 2023, the Gilbert & George Centre opened in East London, a permanent and free-for-all archive.

> *"We became the art. We are it!*
> *We don't have to do anything. We don't*
> *have to scratch, or do something. We are it.*
> *Even when we walk to dinner, we are it."*

"Comedy is a tool of togetherness. It's a way of putting your arm around someone, pointing at something, and saying, 'Isn't it funny that we do that?'"

KATE MCKINNON

Born 1984, United States

A master of impressions, you might best know Kate McKinnon for her work as other people, including Justin Bieber, Ruth Bader Ginsburg, Angela Merkel and, most famously, Hillary Clinton. As a cast member on *SNL* from 2012 to 2022, Kate's hilarious impressions made her one of the show's biggest stars, going on to lead blockbuster comedies *Ghostbusters* and *Rough Night*, and TV shows like Tiger King drama *Joe vs. Carole*.

While rarely commenting on her private life, Kate's sexuality has never been a secret: after all, her first TV gig was on LGBTQIA+ network Logo's *The Big Gay Sketch Show*. On joining *SNL*, Kate made history as the show's first publicly out queer female cast member – and in the process, brought a queer sensibility and lesbian visibility to one of the world's leading comedy stages.

Whether with a pitch-perfect parody of Ellen DeGeneres or original characters like '70s Chicago cop Les Dykawitz, Kate embraced her queerness on-screen and helped rejuvenate the long-running sketch show. Since Kate, *SNL* has added multiple queer cast members, including Bowen Yang, Punkie Johnson and Molly Kearney.

AND ONE MORE THING ...

McKinnon is a proud cat lady, naming her "baby" Nino Positano after the pizza restaurant where he was found. Nino has even appeared in a few *SNL* sketches!

LIL NAS X

Born 1999, United States

When Montero Hill – aka Lil Nas X – paid US$30 for a trap beat with a country twang that he found online while sleeping on his sister's floor, there was no way he knew it would catapult him to superstardom at just 20 years old.

After blowing up on TikTok, "Old Town Road" sat at #1 on the US *Billboard* Hot 100 chart for a record-breaking 19 weeks in 2019. Before that, however, it was disqualified from the Hot Country chart, reigniting a decades-old debate about the erasure of Black artists from the genre. Taking the controversy in stride, Lil Nas challenged the (just plain false) idea that country belongs to white, straight artists. Not only did a remix recorded with Billy Ray Cyrus prove his country chops, but Lil Nas also came out as gay while his song sat strong at #1 – a brave move as the first artist to come out while at the top of any music chart, as Reuters reported at the time.

Since then, Lil Nas X has tackled homophobia and racism head-on with unapologetically Black and queer works. A master of memes and pop culture, Lil Nas always pushes back with irreverence and humour, whether that's by twerking on the devil in music videos or by trolling homophobes who criticise his iconic fashion moments.

Alongside the recent mainstream breakthroughs of other queer Black rappers like Kevin Abstract, Doja Cat, Tyler, the Creator and Frank Ocean (see page 105), Lil Nas's success suggests a world shifting for the better.

AND ONE MORE THING ...
Before he was famous, Lil Nas ran a popular Nicki Minaj fan Twitter, @NasMaraj.

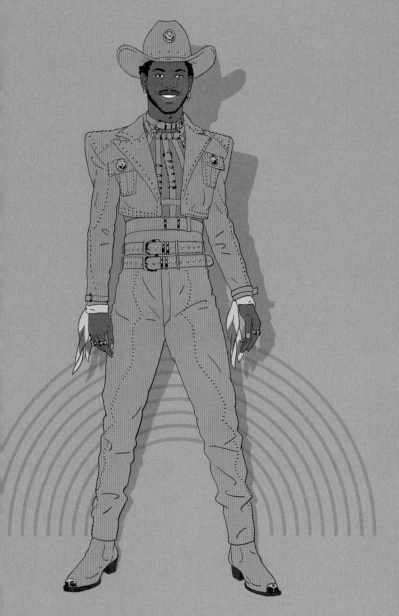

"I try to never throw stones,
but if somebody throws one at me,
I'm throwing an entire house."

"Closed minds are a disorder of the highest order."

HANNAH GADSBY

Born 1978, Australia

In 2017, Hannah Gadsby announced mid-set that they were quitting comedy. At 40, and after more than a decade of stand-up, they were tired of turning their trauma as a genderqueer lesbian with autism into a punchline.

Then, in 2018, that set was released as a Netflix special. Almost overnight, *Nanette* transformed Gadsby from one of Australia's hidden gems to one of the world's most acclaimed comedians. Raw and searing with anger and exhaustion at a patriarchal world, *Nanette* was celebrated as a cathartic work for the #MeToo era that shook up what mainstream comedy could be: heartbreaking and funny at once. Thankfully, Gadsby promptly un-retired.

Paving the way for a new era of convention-breaking comedy, *Nanette* and Gadsby's subsequent specials, *Douglas* and *Body of Work* (plus bestselling memoir *Ten Steps to Nanette*), have inspired countless comedians and queer people to tell their stories in their own way.

Exploring heavy topics without compromise, Gadsby's comedy draws from their own experiences with mental health, homelessness and hatred, having grown up in Tasmania in the '80s and '90s during a time of violent homophobia. But it also celebrates the superpowers of queerness and neurodivergence as ways of experiencing the world.

AND ONE MORE THING ...

Prior to world fame, Gadsby played a character based on themselves in *Please Like Me*, the acclaimed four-season TV show by fellow LGBTQIA+ Aussie comedian Josh Thomas.

KEITH HARING

1958–1990, United States

Responsible for some of the most instantly recognisable artworks of the 20th century, Keith Haring's pop-art murals, drawings and cartoons are a vessel of warmth, empathy and activism. In the '70s, he moved to New York from Pennsylvania and began graffitiing the subway, often using blank advertising spaces as a canvas and creating up to 40 works a day.

With his repeated use of figures the Radiant Baby and Barking Dog, Haring's star rose fast and furiously. Despite his fame, he remained devoted to public work, muralling across the globe (often illegally) and handing out free prints, pins and more.

Much of Haring's art was created in response to the HIV/AIDS epidemic. As an openly gay man working in New York's queer art community, he worked with health authorities to create art promoting safe sex and challenging stigma. Full of life, colour and humour, his art was a beacon of light against morbid and difficult topics, with works also tackling apartheid and crack cocaine use.

In 1988, Haring was diagnosed with AIDS, and shortly after founded the Keith Haring Foundation, supporting AIDS organisations and children's programs. He passed away at 31 years old, with his art continuing to inspire millions.

AND ONE MORE THING ...
You'll probably see Haring's art all the time on clothing.
It's an extension of his Pop Shop, a Warholian-inspired store
to make his work affordable to all.

"Art should be something that liberates your soul, provokes the imagination and encourages people to go further."

"*Normal is not something to aspire to,
it's something to get away from.*"

JODIE FOSTER

Born 1962, United States

One of America's most respected actors, Jodie Foster has been honing her craft since she was just three years old. After a set of Disney films, at age 12 she starred in *Taxi Driver* as child prostitute Iris, a controversial role that saw her nominated for an Academy Award for Best Supporting Actress.

Shaking off the child-actor curse, Foster continued to impress in her twenties with emotionally mature, psychologically taut performances, winning Academy Awards for both legal drama *The Accused* in 1988 and *The Silence of the Lambs* in 1991. Since then, she's continued to ignite the screen in films including *Contact*, *Panic Room* and *Flightplan*, while also directing the likes of *Little Man Tate* and *The Beaver,* as well as episodes of *Black Mirror* and *Orange is the New Black*.

Notoriously private (particularly after her stalker, inspired by *Taxi Driver*, attempted to assassinate then-president Ronald Reagan in 1981 as a misguided way to impress her), Foster did not publicly address her sexuality until 2013. Despite this, her 1993–2008 relationship with film producer Cydney Bernard, who she has two children with, was an open secret. In 2014, she married photographer Alexandra Hedison.

AND ONE MORE THING ...

Foster graduated *magna cum laude* in 1985 from Yale University, with a thesis on novelist Toni Morrison.

GEORGE TAKEI

Born 1937, United States

Best known for playing Lieutenant Sulu over the decades in sci-fi saga *Star Trek*, George Takei has used his status as an adored figure to continually speak out against hatred and bigotry.

Born to two Japanese parents in Los Angeles, Takei spent his early childhood in internment camps following the bombing of Pearl Harbor alongside 125,000 other Japanese immigrants and Japanese American citizens. Eager to act, he landed small parts until *Star Trek* in 1966, at a time when Asian actors were largely cast as one-dimensional villains.

Passionate about injustices, Takei protested the Vietnam War and dabbled in politics but felt unable to come out as a gay man. At the same time, he didn't hide his involvement in gay clubs and societies, and his sexuality was something of an open secret among Trekkies.

In 2005, he came out at 68 years old in response to the then Californian governor Arnold Schwarzenegger vetoing same-sex marriage legislation. He's since been a vocal figure for both LGBTQIA+ and immigration rights with impassioned speeches, viral videos and more than a few dad jokes on Facebook. In 2008, he married Brad Altman, who he had been with since 1985.

AND ONE MORE THING ...
Takei has led multiple productions of *Allegiance*, a 2012 musical inspired by his time in internment camps.

"It's really hard to hate someone for being different when you're too busy laughing together."

"To deny our impulses is to deny the very thing that makes us human."

THE WACHOWSKIS

Born 1965 & 1967, United States

Best known as the sisters behind the revolutionary Matrix film series, the Wachowskis created a billion-dollar universe that, underneath the sci-fi skin and mind-bending slowmo action scenes, explores trans joy and liberation – even if they didn't quite realise it at the time.

"[It] was all about the desire for transformation, but it was all coming from a closeted point of view," Lilly said in an interview with Netflix in 2020. "We were always living in a world of imagination. That's why I gravitated towards sci-fi and fantasy ..."

The series, which began in 1999, follows Neo (Keanu Reeves), a hacker who awakens to destiny and world-warping strength when he learns his world is a simulation. Many trans fans saw their story in *The Matrix* – of the power of finding your true reality – and when the sisters came out publicly as trans women, Lana in 2008 and Lilly in 2016, they felt validated.

Translating the trans experience into a blockbuster beloved by millions is no small feat, but Lilly and Lana have gone on to make equally ambitious works on both technical (*Cloud Atlas*) and thematic levels (*Sense8*). And don't sleep on *Bound* – their directorial debut before *The Matrix*, an ultra-sexy, super-stylish lesbian neo-noir!

AND ONE MORE THING ...

In recent years, the sisters have worked separately, with Lana writing and directing 2021's *The Matrix Resurrections* without Lilly, who was busy co-writing TV series *Work in Progress*.

SYLVIA RIVERA

1951–2002, United States

An essential voice for trans rights, Sylvia Rivera refused to be excluded by the mainstream gay rights movement as a trans Latina woman. Instead, she used her anger as a powerful tool for change.

Born in New York City, Rivera had a difficult childhood, running away from her grandmother's home at age 10. Engaging in sex work to survive, she found friendship and support from community leader Marsha P Johnson (see page 9). Rivera used lots of terms to describe her gender identity, though settled on the now commonly used term "trans woman".

While Johnson's and Rivera's level of involvement in the 1969 Stonewall Riots is contentious (including in their own accounts), their contributions go well beyond that day. In 1970, Rivera and Johnson co-founded STAR, one of the world's first transgender and homeless youth housing organisations. Only 19 herself, Rivera became a mother to many. While STAR was short-lived, Rivera's activism and care was not.

Over the decades and while facing her own adversities, she worked tirelessly to force mainstream LGBTQIA+ advocacy groups to address the discrimination that queer people of colour and trans people faced.

Rivera died at age 50 in 2002 from complications related to liver cancer. That year, the Sylvia Rivera Law Project was founded, offering legal aid to trans, intersex or gender non-conforming people of colour.

AND ONE MORE THING ...

When Rivera was denied from speaking at a 1973 gay liberation rally, she took the stage anyway to a booing crowd, refusing to stay silent and searing with anger at her so-called community.

"*We have to be visible. We are not ashamed of who we are.*"

"... *life is far too important a thing ever to talk seriously about it.*"

OSCAR WILDE

1854–1900, Ireland

Look up "wit" or "raconteur" in the dictionary, and you should find a picture of Oscar Wilde wearing a dramatic fur coat. Born in Dublin but fleeing to London for a more fashionable life, Wilde became a literary celebrity, known not just for his writing, but his delightful charm and flamboyance. His play *The Importance of Being Earnest* and novel *The Picture of Dorian Gray* are regarded to be among our greatest satires, remaining ever-relevant as funny and bold critiques of vanity and decadence.

The latter half of Wilde's life was significantly less glamorous, as he was persecuted for his queerness. While married, Wilde had a number of affairs with men, including with Lord Alfred Douglas, whose powerful father accused Wilde of sodomy, a crime, in 1895. In retaliation, Wilde sued for libel before dropping the case when it was clear several men would testify against him.

This led to his own imprisonment for two years for "gross indecency". After leaving prison in 1897, he lived briefly with Douglas in Naples before Douglas's parents threatened to cut him off. Wilde lived his last years in Paris as a penniless social pariah before dying of meningitis at age 46.

AND ONE MORE THING ...

In 2017, Wilde was posthumously pardoned by the English courts alongside more than 50,000 men who'd been previously charged for homosexual acts – including Alan Turing (see page 89), who the law is informally named after.

FRIDA KAHLO

1907–1954, Mexico

While now celebrated as one of Mexico's great artists and an Indigenous feminist icon, Frida Kahlo's life was spent largely without accolades and with great pain. As a young child, Kahlo contracted polio, leaving her ill for the rest of her life, compounded by a near-fatal bus crash when she was 18. Living with chronic pain, Kahlo had more than 30 corrective surgeries and long periods of bed rest throughout her life.

Kahlo began painting in 1925 while on bed rest, using a custom easel that allowed her to paint while lying down. A mirror also hung over the bed, allowing her to paint the vivid, imaginative self-portraits that are beloved today.

Exploring selfhood and experiences of gender, Kahlo was an avowed communist who centred her politics, identity and Indigenous heritage in her life and art. She proudly performed her multiplicities in her portraits and everyday appearance, alternating between wearing colourful, feminine folk dresses and suits with pulled-back hair, resembling, at times, a drag king.

Twice married to fellow painter Diego Rivera, the two had a tumultuous relationship with many affairs. Openly bisexual, Kahlo had relationships with women, among them Josephine Baker (see page 86), as well as painters Georgia O'Keeffe and Jacqueline Lamba.

AND ONE MORE THING ...

Kahlo was born, lived and died in the same house in Mexico City. It's called La Casa Azul, aka "The Blue House", after the colour of its walls, and is now a museum dedicated to the artist.

"They thought I was a surrealist, but I wasn't. I never painted dreams. I painted my own reality."

> "My choices in life have been unconventional, and that's my business. But I do want to live responsibly and truthfully without hiding."

SARAH PAULSON

Born 1974, United States

An actor's actor, Sarah Paulson throws herself fearlessly into each and every role – whether that be a two-headed circus performer, the sadistic Nurse Ratched or whatever other twisted, complicated and camp character long-time collaborator Ryan Murphy cooks up for her.

After growing up in New York with her single mother, Sarah entered acting immediately after high school. While appearing steadily across stage and screen from the '90s to '00s, she first gained mainstream recognition in 2011 with *American Horror Story*, created by Murphy. While the two previously crossed paths when she worked on *Nip/Tuck*, they've been almost inseparable since, with Sarah appearing in not just *Horror Story* but also *Ratched* and *The People v. O.J. Simpson: American Crime Story*, for which she won a Golden Globe and an Emmy for portraying OJ Simpson prosecutor Marcia Clark. Outside of her work with Murphy, she's starred in acclaimed films such as *12 Years a Slave*, *Carol* and *Ocean's 8*.

Since 2015, Sarah has been in a relationship with actor Holland Taylor, who is 32 years older. The two make for an iconic queer Hollywood couple, often breaking the internet when they walk the red carpet together.

AND ONE MORE THING ...

Despite her talents, Paulson doesn't like watching her own TV shows or films, and tries to avoid it as much as she can!

LENA WAITHE

Born 1984, United States

Lena Waithe lifts people up. As a writer, producer and actor, she works tirelessly to ensure that more queer, Black and diverse stories are being told.

Raised in Chicago, Lena always wanted to be a TV writer. Moving to Los Angeles in her twenties, her breakthrough came in 2015, being cast as Denise on Aziz Ansari's Netflix comedy *Master of None*. Originally white and straight, the character was rewritten to reflect Waithe's experience as a butch Black lesbian – a perspective sorely missing from TV and film. Moving into co-writing the show, Waithe won an Emmy for "Thanksgiving", an episode about Denise's complicated relationship with her family, inspired by her own life.

Continually behind thought-provoking work shining a light on Black and queer experience, her credits include TV drama about South Side Chicago *The Chi*, thriller film *Queen & Slim* and provocative horror anthology *Them*. And while filmmakers like Cheryl Dunye, the first Black lesbian to direct a film with 1996's *The Watermelon Woman*, came before, Waithe's mainstream success marks a watershed for representation. And she's making it easier for emerging diverse artists by producing their work, and with Rising Voices, her development program for marginalised creatives.

AND ONE MORE THING ...

Waithe made history in 2020 when she voiced lesbian cyclops cop Specter in *Onward*, the first openly LGBTQIA+ character in an animated Disney film.

"*The things that make us different –
those are our superpowers.*"

"*Glamour is something more than what you pu[t] on your body. It has to do with the way you carr[y] yourself and the impact you have on others.*"

TOM FORD

Born 1961, United States

Decades before he revitalised Gucci, launched his own fashion label and helped push the fashion world to be more provocative and irreverent, Tom Ford spent his childhood in Texas and New Mexico before moving to New York.

While studying interior design and architecture at the esteemed Parsons School of Design, Ford realised his true love was fashion. With charm (and a few white lies on his résumé), he worked his way into the industry. In 1986, he fell for his future husband, fashion journalist Richard Buckley, who sadly passed away in 2021.

In 1990, he was scouted by a near-insolvent Gucci, and moved to Italy. Soon promoted to Creative Director, Ford's scandalous Gucci G-strings and ultra-suggestive ads turned around their fortunes, even amid countless controversies. When Gucci purchased Yves Saint Laurent in 1999, he became Creative Director of both legendary fashion houses. By the time he left in 2004, Gucci Group was worth US$10 billion.

In addition to founding his own label in 2005, which he sold to Estée Lauder in 2022 for US$2.8 billion, Ford is also an acclaimed filmmaker, having directed and written two critically acclaimed films: *A Single Man* in 2009, and *Nocturnal Animals* in 2016.

AND ONE MORE THING ...

In the '70s, Ford was a regular at New York's legendary Studio 54 – the club's disco glamour and hedonism have been a source of inspiration throughout his career.

RUPAUL

Born 1960, United States

Don't call RuPaul Charles a drag queen! She prefers the title of the "queen of drag", and why shouldn't she? Not only has she turned a misunderstood and maligned art form into a mainstream phenomenon with reality TV hit *RuPaul's Drag Race* – she's opened minds and hearts across the globe to queer people with her own charisma, uniqueness, nerve and talent.

Charles began exploring "gender-fuck" drag as a teenager in Atlanta, go-go dancing and performing in punk bands at clubs. Moving to New York at 17, she adopted the Glamazonian aesthetic we know today, reaching a towering six feet nine inches in heels. Her first brush with fame came in 1989 when leading the conga line in The B-52's music video for "Love Shack", but it was "Supermodel (You Better Work)", her own campy house track, that saw her star catapult in 1993.

Across the '90s, Charles broke new ground constantly, whether with her music, film and TV appearances, a MAC Cosmetics campaign, or her daytime talk show, *The RuPaul Show*. And in 2009, she sashayed onto TV to find America's next drag superstar. The rest is herstory, with 24 Emmys, 20+ US seasons (including *All Stars*) and 15 international editions – and counting!

AND ONE MORE THING ...

RuPaul isn't a stage name! She was named after her mother's love of roux, a soup/stew base in Southern and French cooking.

"You're born naked
and the rest is drag."

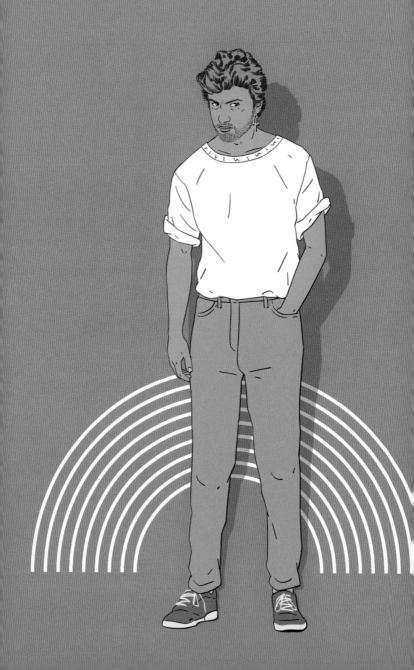

GEORGE MICHAEL

1963–2016, England

Cheeky, provocative and political, George Michael isn't just an all-time bestselling artist behind irresistible hits "Freedom! '90" and "Faith". During his 53 years on Earth, he threw up a finger to conservatives, refusing to be shamed for being an unapologetically sexual gay man.

In the '80s, Michael rose to fame as one-half of Wham!, with mega-hits "Wake Me Up Before You Go-Go", "Last Christmas" and "Careless Whisper". In 1987, he released his debut solo album *Faith*, followed by four more chart-topping albums in the '90s and '00s. During this period, Michael's sexuality was under constant speculation. He was effectively outed in 1998 when he was arrested for cruising by an undercover cop – a controversy he made fun of with his comeback single "Outside".

Throughout his life, Michael was an avid philanthropist, with the proceeds of several of his hits, including "Don't Let the Sun Go Down on Me" and "Last Christmas", going to charities. Only after his death did we learn of the depths of his generosity, as people shared his previously anonymous donations, including covering a game show contestant's IVF treatment, and giving a bartender £5,000 after learning of her student debt.

AND ONE MORE THING ...

In 1985, Wham! was the first Western pop act to tour China.

CLEA DUVALL

Born 1977, United States

In 1999 camp classic *But I'm a Cheerleader*, Clea DuVall plays Graham, a confident, sarcastic lesbian teen at a gay conversion therapy camp. While an awakening for so many queer women, the role was difficult for DuVall, who was out to friends and family but not the world. Having now shared her truth, she's making proudly and defiantly queer work, offering the representation she didn't have growing up.

DuVall entered acting as a teenager, training at a performing arts school in Los Angeles before landing roles in '90s hits *Girl, Interrupted*, *She's All That* and *Can't Hardly Wait*. But after *Cheerleader*, DuVall intentionally avoided public scrutiny – while her credits continued to stack in the '00s, she declined interviews and press.

In 2016, DuVall came out as a lesbian, and a period of creative rejuvenation followed, writing and directing two films: *The Intervention*, where she plays a lesbian alongside *Cheerleader* co-star Natasha Lyonne, and *Happiest Season*, a semi-autobiographical film starring Kristen Stewart about the difficulties of returning home for Christmas as a queer person. She's also recently directed and co-created *High School*, a TV adaptation of the memoir by Canadian queer twin singer-songwriters Tegan and Sara.

AND ONE MORE THING ...

You can see a baby-faced DuVall in the first season of *Buffy the Vampire Slayer*, as a high-schooler so unpopular she starts turning invisible!

"*So much pain comes from not accepting yourself for who you are.*"

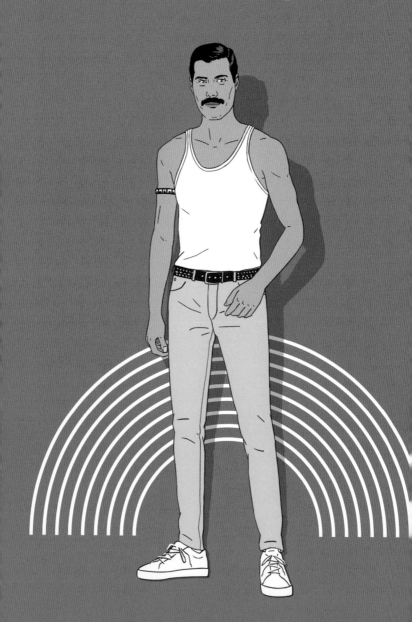

"*The most important thing is to live a fabulous life. As long as it's fabulous, I don't care how long it is.*"

FREDDIE MERCURY

1946–1991, Tanzania

Flamboyant, beyond talented and a singular stage presence, Freddie Mercury will forever be remembered for his out-of-this-world flair and four-octave vocal range.

Born as Farrokh Bulsara to Parsi parents, Mercury spent his childhood between Zanzibar (now part of Tanzania), India and England, landing in London as an adult. Studying art and graphic design, Mercury fronted a set of bands before joining Smile in 1970 – shortly after, he adopted his moniker and renamed the band Queen.

Alongside guitarist Brian May, drummer Roger Taylor and bassist John Deacon, Mercury quickly ruled the world. By the mid '70s, Queen was filling stadiums with hits "We Will Rock You", "We Are the Champions" and opera-rock epic "Bohemian Rhapsody". To this day, Mercury's live performances are legendary, with a unique ability to be over the top and completely sincere at once. Just check out footage of their 1985 Live Aid performance for proof of Mercury's immense power onstage.

Despite his camp demeanour, Mercury never came out publicly. Throughout his life, he dated both men and women, and in private circles referred to long-term partner Jim Hutton as his husband. Diagnosed with AIDS in 1987, Mercury passed away four years later of AIDS-related complications, aged 45.

AND ONE MORE THING ...

In 2018, Mercury was portrayed by Rami Malek in box-office smash biopic *Bohemian Rhapsody*, which was criticised for erasing Mercury's queerness.

JAMES BALDWIN

1924–1987, United States

One of the 20th century's most celebrated writers and thinkers, James Baldwin continues to shape our conceptions of sexuality and race today.

Born in Harlem, Baldwin moved to France as a 24-year-old to live a life less restrained by racism, poverty and homophobia. He spent most of his life there, returning to the US during the height of the Civil Rights Movement.

Prolific and produced with furious speed, Baldwin's essays, novels and plays remain as searing and powerful as when they were first published – a maelstrom of fury, frustration and sadness with the African American experience. Despite his vital voice, Baldwin's sexuality and socialist views saw him distanced from the mainstream Civil Rights Movement, wary of being too radical.

Throughout his life, Baldwin pursued both men and women and was reluctant to categorise his sexuality: in 1965, he said, "If one's to live at all, one's certainly got to get rid of labels." He's perhaps best known for essay collection *Notes of a Native Son* or novella *Giovanni's Room*. Released in 1956 – a full decade before the gay liberation movement took form – it's a bisexual love story of two men, detailing the agony of being unable to live truthfully.

AND ONE MORE THING ...

When he died of cancer in 1987, Baldwin left behind an unfinished manuscript, adapted into 2016 documentary manifesto *I Am Not Your Negro*, narrated by Samuel L Jackson.

"Love takes off the masks we fear
we cannot live without and know
we cannot live within."

"*Lock up your libraries if you like; but there is no gate, no lock, no bolt that you can set upon the freedom of my mind.*"

VIRGINIA WOOLF

1882–1941, England

A titan of literary modernism, Virginia Woolf broke tradition both on the page and in her life. Born into an affluent London society, Woolf was a founding member of the Bloomsbury Group, an intellectual consort guided by modernism, which was a rejection of religion-based ethics and artistic convention in favour of pushing language and society forward.

As a writer, Woolf is celebrated for pioneering stream of consciousness, a narrative style echoing our loose, erratic internal monologues. With novels *Mrs Dalloway*, *To the Lighthouse* and *The Waves*, she used an experimental, enveloping narrative style to capture the frustrations of moving through a patriarchal world.

She's best known for scathing feminist essay *A Room of One's Own* and novel *Orlando*, an epic "biography" following a gender-shifting, immortal figure. The protagonist is inspired by the life of Vita Sackville-West, Woolf's fellow writer and long-term lover. While married to Leonard Woolf, Virginia had several affairs with women.

Throughout her life, Woolf struggled with her mental health as detailed in her writing, and died by suicide at age 59. While some of her beliefs on race and class do not hold up today, Woolf remains vital in shaping literature and feminism as we know it.

AND ONE MORE THING ...

The Hours, an acclaimed 2002 drama directed by Stephen Daldry, depicts Woolf while writing *Mrs Dalloway*. It was nominated for nine Academy Awards, with Nicole Kidman winning Best Actress for her portrayal of the writer.

DAVID SEDARIS

Born 1956, United States

Sardonic, sharp and delightfully odd, David Sedaris is a humorist, essayist and comedian whose off-kilter view of the world has entertained and moved millions. Across his books, plays, articles and radio performances, Sedaris digs into everyday experiences and taboos alike, revealing just how delightfully strange and silly life, family and strangers can be.

Raised in North Carolina with five siblings (including sister Amy, an equally hilarious comedian and frequent collaborator), Sedaris spent his twenties trying to make it as a visual and performance artist. It was a period largely of failure, odd jobs and drug addiction, as outlined in his diaries, which he has written daily since 1977.

In the mid '80s, he was discovered by radio host Ira Glass while reading diary entries in a club. This led to his big break reading *Santaland Diaries* on NPR in 1992, a story about his humiliating experiences as a Christmas elf. Since then, he's published more than 10 essay and story collections, including *Naked* and *Me Talk Pretty One Day*, and diary compilations *Theft by Finding* and *A Carnival of Snackery*. Sedaris has been sober since 1999, and lives mostly in rural England with his long-time partner, painter Hugh Hamrick.

AND ONE MORE THING ...
Sedaris's home of West Sussex named a garbage truck after him, the "Pig Pen Sedaris", for his habit of picking up street litter late at night while wearing a headlight.

"I was a smart-ass, born and raised. This had been my curse and would continue to be so."

"When life gives you lemons don't make lemonade, make pink lemonade. Be unique."

WANDA SYKES

Born 1964, United States

One of the world's most successful comedians, Wanda Sykes has made it in an industry historically averse to who she is: a queer Black woman. Best known for her scene-stealing roles in sitcoms like *The New Adventures of Old Christine* and *Curb Your Enthusiasm*, Sykes has worked behind the scenes to make comedy more diverse, while also routinely using her wit to turn racism, homophobia and sexism into the butt of a joke.

Raised by a banker mum and an army colonel dad, Sykes started stand-up in the '80s on the side of her first job: working for US intelligence at the National Security Agency. After opening for Chris Rock, she earned a writing slot on his show in the '90s, before landing her own special and sitcom in 2003 – the first of many to come, including *The Wanda Sykes Show*.

Outspoken and passionate about civil rights, Sykes came out as a lesbian while protesting the anti–same sex marriage Proposition 8, revealing she was married to interior designer Alex Niedbalski. She's also used her platform to support Black Lives Matter, as well as speak out against trans discrimination. Recently, Sykes starred in sitcom *The Other Two*, animated series *Q-Force*, and *The Upshaws*, which she also co-created.

SAM SMITH

Born 1992, England

Sam Smith's meteoric rise – from an unknown powerhouse vocal on 2012 Disclosure banger "Latch" to our biggest non-binary pop star – is due to the power of someone embracing who they truly are, while being unafraid to grow and change.

With undeniable talent (that falsetto!), Smith's 2014 debut album *In the Lonely Hour* reached #1 in several countries, including the UK and Australia, when they were just 22. Once the world was singing along to their heartbreak ballads, they came out as a gay man. In the years since, Smith has come out twice more: first, as genderqueer in 2017, then non-binary in 2019, helping to show the wider world that identity is fluid and not always a linear journey. In the process, they evolved from "the male Adele", as the press called them, to the boundary-pushing provocateur behind music videos with golden showers and transgressive worldwide hit "Unholy", a duet with trans pop star Kim Petras.

With an irreverent and unapologetic fashion sense, Sam has repeatedly been the target of fat shaming within the queer community. While fighting against this toxic standard, they're honest about their fluctuating sense of body positivity, reminding us that self-esteem isn't a one-way journey – even for a superstar.

AND ONE MORE THING ...

In 2023 for "Unholy", Smith became the first openly non-binary artist to win a Grammy Award.

*"I didn't become successful until
I became myself."*

_"I would rather be a bad feminist
than no feminist at all."_

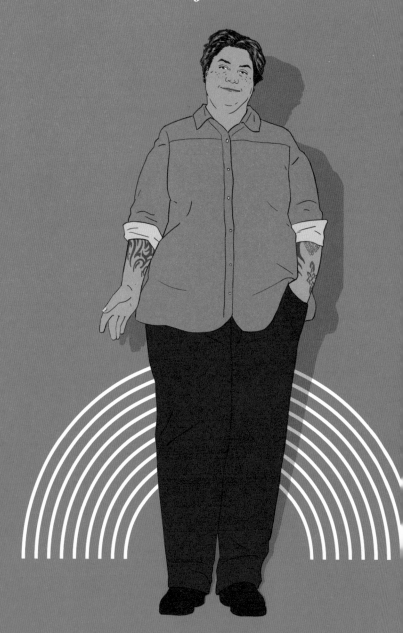

ROXANE GAY

Born 1974, United States

With her earth-shattering words, Roxane Gay has helped transform how we think about race, bodies, sexuality, violence and feminism. Best known for her essay collection *Bad Feminist*, Gay's writing never shies away from daunting topics, and always doing so with honesty, empathy and nuance.

As per her memoir *Hunger*, Gay breaks her life into "before" and "after": a relatively happy childhood in Nebraska raised by Haitian immigrants changed when she was gang raped at age 12. Keeping it a secret, she developed various issues around eating, weight gain and self-esteem. A bright mind and writer, she entered academia, completing a PhD in 2010, and the year after published her first book, *Ayiti*.

It was *Bad Feminist* that made Gay a household name in her thirties, a 2014 collection of new and previously viral essays about pop culture, race, food, abuse, violence and more. Fearless, furious and witty, her writing helped shape contemporary feminist thought, pushed further with books *Difficult Women*, *Not That Bad* and harrowing memoir *Hunger*, as well as her opinion column in *The New York Times*. In 2020, she eloped with fellow writer Debbie Millman.

AND ONE MORE THING ...
Gay's credits also include *World of Wakanda*, a six-part *Black Panther* comic spin-off.

JONATHAN VAN NESS

Born 1987, United States

As a self-care guru, hairstylist and the cheerleader we all need, Jonathan Van Ness knows the power of a makeover. Finding fame in 2018 as the grooming expert on Netflix's hugely successful reboot of *Queer Eye*, the world fell in love with JVN's uplifting outlook.

Proudly loud, non-binary and flamboyant, JVN – sometimes called "gay Jesus" by fans because of his long locks – encourages makeover subjects struggling with self-confidence to embrace their own uniqueness and find "pockets of joy" even in difficult situations.

And he's proof it works – growing up in a small Illinois town, Van Ness endured a lot of bigotry as an openly gay and feminine teen, including death threats. On and off the show, JVN has been raw and honest about his own struggles with body issues, addiction, sexual abuse and living with HIV. Having been through a lot and come out as a bastion for self-love, he's able to connect to people who need help and see them without judgement – be sure to keep the tissues handy while watching.

Outside of *Queer Eye*, JVN's published multiple books, including a memoir, hosts a weekly podcast *Getting Curious*, and uses his platform to advocate for LGBTQIA+ rights and social issues.

AND ONE MORE THING ...

Before *Queer Eye*, Van Ness hosted a popular *Game of Thrones* recap series called *Gay of Thrones* – and even received an Emmy nomination for it!

"I want people to fall in love with themselves and to be really proud and full of joy for the space they take up."

"I think when I am dressed up I reach more people than a painting in a gallery."

LEIGH BOWERY

1961–1994, Australia

Endlessly referenced, never replicated, Leigh Bowery's avant-garde club nights, outrageous designs and transgressive performances are simply legendary.

Born in the small Melbourne suburb of Sunshine, Bowery's artistic ambitions saw him move to London at 19, selling clothes at Kensington Market and soon rising the ranks in the New Romantic club scene. Proudly freakish, his handmade outfits, giant dresses and "facekinis" were both beautiful and a touch frightening. He was, in many ways, a spiritual precursor to the Club Kids of '90s New York.

But Bowery really made his name with Taboo, a club night that became its own venue in 1985. A site of debauchery, sexual hedonism and visceral performance art, Taboo lived up to its name. Bowery's most famous performance saw him "birth" long-term partner Nicola Bateman onstage. Hidden beneath his outfit and strapped to his belly upside-down, she would emerge in a show of fake blood and umbilical-cord sausages.

Bowery died of AIDS-related illness at just 33 – a shock to all, as he didn't tell anyone he was HIV positive, despite being diagnosed six years prior. In his last years, he fronted glam-pop group Minty, and despite being gay, married Bateman in a "personal art performance".

AND ONE MORE THING ...

Bowery was a muse of painter Lucian Freud, whose portraits of Bowery are considered some of his best works.

CARA DELEVINGNE

Born 1992, England

Model, actor and verified It Girl of the 2010s, Cara Delevingne is always herself – goofy, outspoken and unapologetic. Growing up in London in a wealthy family, she followed older sister Poppy's footsteps and entered modelling as a teen. Becoming one of the most in-demand names with her trademark bushy brows, she was awarded Model of the Year at the British Fashion Awards not just once, but twice, in 2012 and 2014.

After conquering the fashion world, Delevingne stepped away from the catwalk to focus on acting, landing the lead in teen romance *Paper Towns*. She's continued to light up screens with roles in blockbusters like *Suicide Squad*, indie dramas like *Her Smell* and TV hits like *Carnival Row* and *Only Murders in the Building*. She's also the author of *Mirror, Mirror*, a queer coming-of-age novel.

Throughout her career, Delevingne has used her celebrity to advocate and educate on a variety of social causes – whether being open about her pansexuality, coming out as gender fluid in 2018, or speaking candidly about her experiences with depression and ADHD. She also joined a chorus of voices in 2017's #MeToo movement, sharing her story of sexual harassment from Harvey Weinstein.

AND ONE MORE THING ...

Delevingne is also a musician, and features in songs by Fiona Apple, Pharrell Williams and ex-girlfriend St Vincent.

"If no-one is listening, shout until they do. Everyone deserves a voice."

"*The worst of times in San Francisco was still better than the best of times anywhere else.*"

ARMISTEAD MAUPIN

Born 1944, United States

Raised by an ultra-conservative family in North Carolina, Armistead Maupin's life and famous book series *Tales of the City* are both tribute to San Francisco and the power of finding queer community.

While now canonised as an influential queer novelist, Maupin's life almost looked very different. Maupin was a proud conservative in his twenties and closeted, pushing down his sexuality to serve in the navy during the Vietnam War. But when he was offered a journalism job in San Francisco, he leapt at the chance, and soon found himself in the sexual liberation of '70s bathhouses. Inspired by his new home, in 1976 Maupin began writing *Tales of the City* as a serial for the *San Francisco Chronicle*.

Centring on the fictional apartments of 28 Barbary Lane, the series follows several queer characters across decades, spanning ten books. Initially written and published quickly, the series incorporated real-world events, celebrity gossip and pop culture as it occurred – the fourth book *Babycakes* is cited as the first fiction to mention AIDS. *Tales of the City* has been adapted multiple times for TV, radio and stage as a musical. Most recently, Murray Bartlett and Elliot Page (see page 70) starred in a Netflix version.

(see page 70)

AND ONE MORE THING ...

Armistead Maupin isn't a pen-name, though it is an anagram of "is a man I dreamt up".

ELTON JOHN

Born 1947, England

One of the bestselling musicians of all time, Sir Elton John's songwriting talents, flamboyant style and huge heart have left an indelible mark on music, culture and millions of lives.

Born Reginald Dwight, the Rocket Man's prodigious piano talents saw him win a scholarship at age 11 to study at the Royal Academy of Music. After playing in band Bluesology as a teen, John went solo with the help of lyricist Bernie Taupin, who has been his lifelong songwriting partner since 1967. The rest is history, with John's ability to master all genres and his over-the-top performances making him a legend. In addition to more than 50 top-40 hits across 30+ albums, Elton also composed the iconic soundtrack for *The Lion King*.

John came out as bisexual in 1976, later clarifying in '92, one marriage later, that he was gay. That same year, he founded the Elton John AIDS Foundation, a non-profit organisation that has raised over US$600 million to support HIV programs across the globe.

John married long-time partner David Furnish in 2014, who he has two sons with. In 2019, his early life was dramatised in the musical biopic *Rocketman*, starring Taron Egerton.

AND ONE MORE THING ...
John's final world tour, Farewell Yellow Brick Road,
spanned more than 300 stadium shows between 2018 and 2023,
and grossed upwards of US$900 million.

"I've only been interested in
the artistic side of life."

"*Whenever anyone has called me a bitch, I have taken it as a compliment.*"

MARGARET CHO

Born 1968, United States

Outrageous, crass and unafraid of ruffling feathers, this bisexual comedian mines her darkest moments to shed light on racism, fatphobia and more.

Born into a Korean American family in San Francisco, Margaret Cho was bullied at school for her race and weight, and was also sexually abused by relatives and family friends. Cho began stand-up after high school, leading to *All-American Girl*, a sitcom based on Cho's life. While a representational landmark as one of the first sitcoms to focus on an East Asian American family, it was criticised for stereotypical, offensive jokes. Cho was miserable and under pressure to drastically lose weight, eventually resulting in kidney failure. After it was cancelled, she fell into substance abuse aided by depression, later writing about the experiences in an award-winning one-woman show and her memoir.

This candour has made Cho a powerful, in-demand comedian – one who uses comedy to cleverly comment on big issues, including anti-Asian hate, and destigmatise conversations around mental health. As an actor, she's stolen scenes in sitcoms like *30 Rock*, *Drop Dead Diva* and *The Flight Attendant*, and shown her range in films like action hit *Face/Off*, cult classic *Bam Bam and Celeste* and queer comedy *Fire Island*.

AND ONE MORE THING ...
In addition to her comedic prowess, Cho is also a musician, podcaster and clothing designer.

ELLIOT PAGE

Born 1987, Canada

Elliot Page might just be one of the most well-known trans men in the world – it was the lack of visibility amid rising anti-trans sentiment that inspired the actor to share his truth in 2020. "I love that I am trans," he wrote in his coming out statement at the time. "And I love that I am queer. And the more I hold myself close and fully embrace who I am, the more I dream, the more my heart grows and the more I thrive."

A beloved and successful actor, Elliot has been in the public eye since he was 10. He broke big in the US in the mid 2000s as superhero Kitty Pryde in *X-Men: The Last Stand* and as the lead in era-defining indie comedy *Juno*, for which he received an Oscar nomination. In 2014, he came out as queer, and began advocating for LGBTQIA+ and human rights through his work.

He and best friend Ian Daniel created *Gaycation*, a two-season docuseries exploring LGBTQIA+ culture and activism across the globe, followed by *There's Something in the Water*, a documentary on environmental racism. Since coming out as a trans man, Elliot has fought against anti-trans legislation, and written a bestselling memoir, *Pageboy*.

AND ONE MORE THING ...

Page came out as a trans man in between filming seasons of Netflix superhero show *The Umbrella Academy* – his character also transitioned off-camera, between seasons.

"This world would be a whole lot better if we just made an effort to be less horrible to one another."

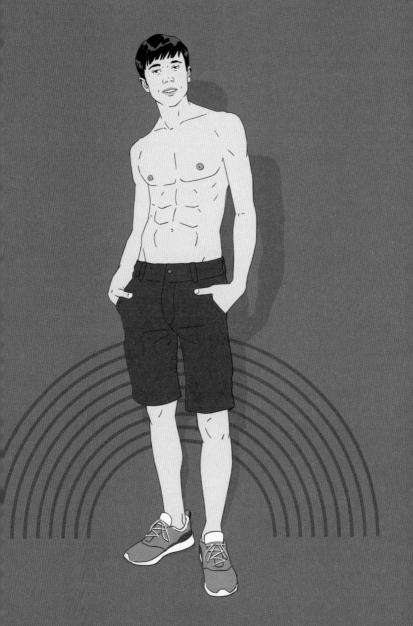

"It is revolutionary for any trans person to choose to be seen and visible in a world that tells us we should not exist."

LAVERNE COX

Born 1972, United States

A trailblazer for trans rights and representation, actress and activist Laverne Cox has too many "firsts" in her career to mention. Drawn to performing her whole life, Cox originally studied creative writing and ballet in her home state of Alabama before moving to New York to pursue acting, where she also began transitioning.

After a spate of small roles and reality TV gigs, including hosting groundbreaking makeover show *TRANSform Me*, Cox first gained global attention for her role on Netflix prison drama *Orange is the New Black* as Sophia Burset, a trans prisoner. At a time when cis male actors were receiving Oscars for "bravely" playing trans characters, Sophia was proof of the power of having trans actors portray (and write) trans characters. It also marked the first time a trans woman of colour had a leading role in a mainstream TV series.

With the show's success, Cox used her platform to be a voice for trans women of colour, educating the masses on the trans experience, racism and how the two intersect. Outside of her successful acting career, Cox has produced multiple documentaries on trans issues, including the Emmy-winning *The T Word*, *Free CeCe!* and *Disclosure*.

AND ONE MORE THING ...

Cox has a twin brother, M Lamar, who played Sophia in *Orange is the New Black*'s pre-transition flashbacks.

LILY TOMLIN

Born 1939, United States

Making the world laugh for more than seven decades, Lily Tomlin has done it all. And she's done it with a distinctly feminist bent, from sticking it to the man alongside Jane Fonda and Dolly Parton in *9 to 5* to carving out a long and successful career in an industry stacked against funny women.

Growing up in Detroit, Tomlin first found a love for performing while acting in a play at Wayne State University, soon dropping out of medicine to pursue comedy. After small stints on variety hours, she appeared on sketch show *Laugh-In* from 1969 to 1973 with beloved characters like brutal telephone operator Ernestine and existential five-year-old Edith Ann.

In 1971, she met Jane Wagner, her lifelong partner and comedy co-writer. While they never officially went public or came out, their relationship was something of an open secret. Over the decades, they worked together on Tomlin's TV specials, plays and most famous character creations.

In addition to *9 to 5*, Tomlin has starred in countless shows and films, including *Nashville*, *The West Wing*, *Will & Grace* and Netflix comedy *Grace and Frankie*, in which she reunited with Jane Fonda.

AND ONE MORE THING ...

Tomlin is the voice of Ms Frizzle, the teacher in children's show *The Magic School Bus*, in both the original and the 2017 reboot!

"I can handle reality in small doses, but as a lifestyle, it's much too confining."

"A rose is a rose is a rose is a rose."

GERTRUDE STEIN

1874–1946, United States

Ask any art and literature lover where they'd like to time travel
to, and there's a good chance they'll say Gertrude Stein's Parisian
salon. Most Saturdays, she'd hold court with the likes of Picasso,
Hemingway, Henri Matisse and F Scott Fitzgerald. But beyond her
legendary parties, Stein is an accomplished writer in her own right –
a boundary-pushing force behind some of the first sapphic love
stories of the 20th century.

Leaving America with her brother Leo in 1902, they became
prominent art collectors in Paris. With an eye for the cutting edge,
they helped promote artists including Renoir, Cézanne, Matisse and
Picasso, who painted a portrait of Stein. In 1907, she met life partner
Alice B Toklas, who was treated in high society as Stein's "wife", and
the narrator of Stein's most famous work, *The Autobiography of Alice
B Toklas*. Despite the name, it is actually Stein's life story.

Her novels *Q.E.D.* and *Tender Buttons* are more explicit with
describing lesbian love affairs. Her 1923 poem *Miss Furr and Miss
Skeene* was one of the first published works to use the word "gay" to
refer to sexuality – in fact, the poem repeats the word more than a
hundred times!

AND ONE MORE THING ...

In their hundreds of love letters, Stein and Toklas had nicknames
for each other: "Baby Precious" for Toklas, and "Mr Cuddle-
Wuddle" for Stein.

QUENTIN CRISP

1908–1999, England

Few can live their entire lives unapologetically, but Quentin Crisp embraced his flamboyance even when it put him at harm. Raised in London at the turn of the century by a wealthy family, Crisp was always himself – an effeminate figure who paraded around with lilac hair and in make-up, blouses and painted nails. Despite repeated public beatings, he never toned it down, working briefly as a rent boy and surrounding himself in a nascent queer community. In the '40s, he began work as a life model, later publishing an autobiography in 1968, *The Naked Civil Servant*. A TV adaptation turned him into a celebrity raconteur on the cusp of entering his seventies.

He began performing one-man shows and acting, most notably appearing as Queen Elizabeth I in the 1992 film adaptation of Virginia Woolf's *Orlando* (see page 49). He published several more books, including *How to Become a Virgin* and *Doing it with Style*.

Despite his popularity as a camp figure, Crisp had a complex relationship with his queerness. He would often deride the gay rights movement and AIDS for a punchline. Before he died at age 90, Crisp began to refer to himself as both a homosexual and a trans woman, continuing to predominantly use he/him pronouns.

AND ONE MORE THING ...
Crisp kept his telephone number publicly listed, and delighted in taking calls from strangers, often accepting dinner invitations.

"Never keep up with the Joneses.
Drag them down to your level.
It's cheaper."

"*I am, at heart, a gentleman.*"

MARLENE DIETRICH

1901–1992, Germany

Androgynous starlet of Hollywood's Golden Age, bisexual icon and outspoken anti-fascist, Marlene Dietrich's private life is as captivating as her magnetic on-screen presence. Born just outside of Berlin, Dietrich was captivated by the city's 1920s cabarets, openly queer nightlife and drag balls.

After starring in one of Germany's first talking films, Dietrich was catapulted to fame when she signed to Paramount Pictures, becoming one of 1930s Hollywood's most recognisable femme fatales. During this period, the Third Reich requested she return to Germany, leading to her publicly denouncing Nazism and becoming a US citizen. In 1947, she was given a Medal of Freedom by the US Government for making more than 500 visits to Allied troops during World War II. Post-war, Dietrich returned to the stage as a cabaret artist, touring the world into her seventies.

A style maverick, Dietrich was fond of men's suits and tuxedos while remaining traditionally beautiful, playing with an androgyny that confused (and excited) audiences. Dietrich was married to Rudolf Sieber from 1923 until his death in 1976 – while she had many affairs with men and women, Sieber was aware of them. Dietrich's dalliances include John F Kennedy, Frank Sinatra, Mercedes de Acosta and countless more women in her "Sewing Circle".

AND ONE MORE THING ...

In 1930 film *Morocco*, a tux-wearing Dietrich gave one of the first on-screen lesbian kisses, in the musical scene she's arguably best remembered for today.

DIVINE

1945–1988, United States

The devilish muse of camp king John Waters, Divine is an icon of bad taste, filthy behaviour and underground queer cinema that still shocks today. Born in Baltimore to a conservative family, Glenn Milstead revelled in rebelling on- and off-screen. Beginning drag to emulate Elizabeth Taylor, Milstead was encouraged by Waters to be equal parts Godzilla and glamazon, nicknaming him Divine.

Starring in 10 Waters films, Divine's diabolic roles include *Female Trouble*'s murderous teen Dawn Davenport, *Hairspray* housewife Edna Turnblad and "the filthiest person alive" Babs Johnson in *Pink Flamingos*. The latter film's revolting end scene, where Divine eats genuine dog poo, turned him and Waters into countercultural stars.

Divine also worked separately from Waters as an actor, disco singer and nightclub performer – often brutally insulting the audience to rapturous laughter. Despite his boundary-pushing persona, Divine was cagey about his queerness in public, and resented that he wasn't taken seriously as an actor out of drag. After being estranged from his family, Divine's mother reached out in 1981, allowing the two to reconcile. At the height of his celebrity and just three weeks after *Hairspray* was released, Divine died aged 42 of heart failure.

AND ONE MORE THING ...

Divine's drag make-up was the main inspiration for Ursula the Sea Witch's look in Disney's 1989 version of *The Little Mermaid*.

*"I think the least of people's worries
is a man in a dress."*

"Art knows no prejudice, art knows no boundaries, art doesn't really have judgement in its purest form."

K.D. LANG

Born 1961, Canada

Country singer Kathryn Dawn Lang was already adored in Canada when the rest of the world caught on. In 1987, crooner Roy Orbison invited lang to duet his classic "Crying", winning the duo a Grammy. Combined with a show-stopping performance at the 1988 Winter Olympic Games' closing ceremony, lang's arresting voice captivated the globe.

While at a new height of fame, lang came out in 1992 on the cover of *The Advocate*, arguably becoming at that moment the world's most visible lesbian. While some country fans took issue, even going so far as to picket her presence at the Grammys, lang's career continued to soar.

Her biggest song "Constant Craving" has seen millions sing along to a tale of lesbian pining. Plus, lang's androgynous suits and "cowpunk" butch style has always kept her queerness front and centre. Let's not forget the iconic photoshoots either, like the cover art of album *Drag* or the sensual 1993 *Vanity Fair* cover where she's in a barber's chair, receiving a shave from Cindy Crawford. Now considering herself "semi-retired", lang has more than 10 albums under her cowboy belt, including collaborations with Tony Bennett, Elton John (see page 66) and more.

AND ONE MORE THING ...

k.d. lang decapitalised her stage name in reference
to poet e.e. cummings.

JOSEPHINE BAKER

1906–1975, United States

Vaudeville legend, civil rights activist, banana-clad fashionista and
World War II spy: what couldn't Josephine Baker do? Born Freda
Josephine McDonald, Baker helped her impoverished family as
a child by dancing for change on Missouri's streets. Her talents
noticed, she entered show business at 15, adopting her stage name
and moving to New York in the early '20s. There, she performed
regularly at the legendary Plantation Club, and was part of the rise
of Black art and culture known as the Harlem Renaissance. Still, like
James Baldwin (see page 46), Baker felt the oppression of America's
enshrined racism, and left for Paris in 1925.

Baker became a star in the jazz-obsessed city thanks to her risqué
"Danse Sauvage" routine, where she would dance in a revealing skirt
made of bananas. Also a talented singer and actor, Baker wowed
audiences across Europe with tours and film roles. During World
War II, Baker worked as a spy in Nazi-occupied Paris by passing on
secrets she overheard.

Returning to the US post-war, Baker refused to perform for
segregated audiences and was an outspoken civil rights activist.
While married to four men throughout her life, Baker had affairs
with several women, allegedly including French novelist Colette and
Mexican artist Frida Kahlo (see page 30).

AND ONE MORE THING ...

Baker made history as a chanteuse in *Zouzou* as the
first Black woman to play a leading role in a major film.

"... I have walked into the palaces of kings and queens and into the houses of presidents. And much more. But I could not walk into a hotel in America and get a cup of coffee, and that made me mad."

"*We can only see a short distance ahead, but we can see plenty there that needs to be done.*"

ALAN TURING

1912–1954, England

A World War II hero often credited as the father of modern-day computer science and AI, Alan Turing showed remarkable mathematic and scientific understanding from a young age.

After studying mathematics, his seminal 1936 paper created the Turing machine, a hypothetical device that became central to modern computation. He later worked on some of the first computers and created the Turing test, which underpins how we think of AI today. During World War II, Turing worked with other scientists on a cipher-breaking machine, allowing Allies to decode up to 84,000 intercepted messages per month, saving countless lives. For his work, he was awarded an OBE.

But in 1952, Turing was charged for "gross indecency" – the same anti-homosexual charge that saw Oscar Wilde (see page 29) imprisoned. Offered the choice of jail or probation with chemical castration, he chose the latter. His clearance for UK intelligence was rescinded, and he was denied entry into the US. Two years later, at 41, he died of cyanide poisoning, potentially a suicide.

Since celebrated for his achievements, in 2013, Queen Elizabeth II pardoned Turing for his "crime". In 2017, the UK retroactively exonerated all men historically convicted of indecency, the act of which informally became known as the Alan Turing law.

AND ONE MORE THING ...
When charged, Turing didn't deny his homosexuality – in fact, he mocked the law as morally wrong.

ANDY WARHOL

1928–1987, United States

Born in Pennsylvania to parents from modern-day Slovakia, pop-art pioneer Andy Warhol was a shy, often sick child who moved to New York in the 1950s to work in advertising.

His first gallery exhibits of his commercial drawings kicked off a career dedicated to eradicating the lines between consumerism, fame and fine art. But in the '60s, Warhol became the artist we know today with silk-screen printing, allowing him to produce work on mass scale. He also moved into The Factory, a legendary studio, art assembly line and endless party scene for creatives and the "superstars" who featured in his films.

In 1968, Warhol was shot by artist Valerie Solanas, who was angry she was being ignored by the star-maker. He would have complications for the rest of his life, and would have to wear a surgical corset. After the assassination attempt, he largely retreated from socialite life but continued making art. He died in 1987 after gallbladder surgery, having never recovered completely from the attack.

Predating the gay liberation movement by a decade, Warhol lived as an openly gay man but struggled with feelings of freakishness. In response, he turned his flamboyance and eccentricities into a performance, wearing wigs and sunglasses almost constantly.

AND ONE MORE THING ...

Warhol's paintings are some of the most expensive artworks ever sold – in 2022, *Shot Sage Blue Marilyn* sold for US$195 million.

"Art is what you can get away with."

"I believe we all have different ways we came to the gay community and we can't and shouldn't [be] pigeonholed into one cultural narrative ..."

CYNTHIA NIXON

Born 1966, United States

Whether you identify as a Carrie, Samantha, Miranda or Charlotte, one thing's for certain: *Sex and the City* wouldn't be the same without Cynthia Nixon. Famous for playing the show's sharp and cynical lawyer Miranda Hobbes, Nixon is also often a voice of reason in real life, too, using her platform to speak out against harmful immigration and anti-LGBTQIA+ policies.

Born and raised in New York, Nixon entered acting as a child, with a successful Broadway career and supporting film roles before landing a role in the culture-defining *Sex and the City* in 1998. Winning an Emmy for Outstanding Supporting Actress for the original show's final season in 2004, she's since returned to the role in two films and sequel series *And Just Like That...* Inspired by Nixon's own queerness, Miranda explores her sexuality in the new series.

Outside of Miranda, Nixon has had many acclaimed roles across film, TV and stage. In 2018, she ran for governor of New York, with a platform addressing income inequality, universal health care, LGBTQIA+ rights and over-policing. While not elected, she continues to advocate on these issues, especially around trans rights, speaking about her own experiences as the proud mother of a trans man.

AND ONE MORE THING ...

Nixon is just an Oscar away from a coveted EGOT, having been awarded two Emmys, a Grammy and two Tony awards.

NEIL PATRICK HARRIS

Born 1973, United States

Neil Patrick Harris is an anomaly – a child actor who went on to eclipse his early fame, moving from strength to strength. After melting hearts for four seasons as the teenage prodigy in *Doogie Howser, M.D.*, Harris successfully made the leap to adult actor across TV, film and theatre.

In 2005, his role as womaniser Barney Stinson in sitcom *How I Met Your Mother* catapulted him to new heights of fame, with his face sold on shirts, mugs and everything else. In 2006, he came out as gay, later revealing he'd been dating fellow actor David Burtka for several years – a bold move while playing a character idolised by straight men across the globe. The two had twins via surrogate in 2010, and were married in 2014.

Since *How I Met Your Mother* ended, Harris has tallied countless credits across film, TV and theatre, from *Gone Girl* to *A Series of Unfortunate Events* and the 2014 Broadway production of *Hedwig and the Angry Inch*, for which he won a Tony Award. As a couple, he and David are avid philanthropists, especially of LGBTQIA+ foundations including the AIDS Healthcare Foundation, Live Out Loud and The Trevor Project.

AND ONE MORE THING ...
An avid magician, Harris is the author of *The Magic Misfits*, a series of young-adult fiction books.

"*Parents need to be more accepting of who their kids are and less concerned about what society thinks they need to be.*"

"For me, life is about being positive and hopeful, choosing to be joyful, choosing to be encouraging, choosing to be empowering."

BILLY PORTER

Born 1969, United States

A quadruple threat, singer, actor, writer and director Billy Porter's star shines bright across Broadway, film, television – and red carpets.

Porter began on Broadway with *Miss Saigon* in 1991, but his breakthrough moment came in 2013, originating the role of *Kinky Boots'* drag lead, Lola. Winning a Tony for Best Actor, Porter credits Lola with opening him to the power of his own femininity, allowing him to shake off the toxic masculinity lingering from growing up in a Pentecostal environment. The wider world fell in love with Porter on *Pose*, Ryan Murphy's series set in New York's ballroom community.

Playing ball emcee Pray Tell, Porter's exuberance leapt off the screen, as did his pain, as Pray dealt with living with HIV. For his powerful performance, Porter won a 2019 Primetime Emmy for Outstanding Lead Actor in a Drama Series – making history as the first openly gay Black man to be nominated for a lead category, let alone win.

Since *Pose*, Porter has starred in blockbusters including *80 for Brady* and 2021's live-action *Cinderella*, and made his directorial debut with *Anything's Possible*. He's also a fashion icon and Met Gala favourite, having learnt from Pray how to turn a look!

AND ONE MORE THING ...

Porter is just an Oscar away from the coveted EGOT, already having won an Emmy, a Grammy and a Tony.

JANET MOCK

Born 1983, United States

Janet Mock didn't set out to be an activist, but has become one of our most vital, impactful voices fighting for trans rights.

Mock began her career as an editor for *People* magazine, with things shifting in 2011 when she shared her experiences as a trans woman of colour for a *Marie Claire* article. Mock was frustrated with the viral article, titled "I Was Born a Boy", explaining that the framing undermined her truth: she was always a girl.

Expanding on this moment, Mock wrote *Redefining Realness*, a 2014 memoir about undergoing her transition as a Black and Kanaka Maoli teen in Hawaii. An international bestseller, the memoir catapulted Mock into a leading figurehead for the trans movement, educating people on the shared experiences of many trans women of colour. She's since followed it up with *Surpassing Certainty*, a memoir of her twenties.

Mock is also a television writer, director and producer, working predominantly with showrunner Ryan Murphy. When she was hired for *Pose*, a drama set in New York's ballroom community of the '80s and '90s, Mock made history as the first openly trans woman of colour to be hired as a TV writer.

AND ONE MORE THING ...
Mock named herself after Janet Jackson.

"I believe that telling our stories, first to ourselves and then to one another and the world, is a revolutionary act."

*"If a bullet should enter my brain,
let that bullet destroy every closet door."*

HARVEY MILK

1930–1978, United States

Harvey Milk's road to making history was anything but straight and narrow. Before he became one of the US's first openly gay public officials, Milk spent the majority of his life closeted and conservative.

Adrift for his first three decades, Milk's worldview shifted after embracing the '60s flower child movement. Soon after, he moved to San Francisco's famed gay hub, the Castro District. Frustrated by the police's treatment of the gay community and encountering government bureaucracy as the co-owner of shopfront Castro Camera, Milk decided to run for city supervisor in 1973. Gaining support over three successive election runs, Milk galvanised the gay community and labour groups, campaigning as the (unofficial) mayor of Castro Street.

In 1977, he was elected, making headlines across the country and receiving death threats. One of his first actions was passing a bill outlawing discrimination based on sexuality. The sole dissenting vote was from Dan White, who assassinated Milk and city mayor George Moscone on 27 November 1978 – just 10 months after Milk was sworn in. His tragic death only further united the gay liberation movement in anger and grief. Today, he is remembered as a martyr for gay rights.

AND ONE MORE THING ...

Prior to politics, Milk served in the US Navy during the Korean War, and was given an "other than honourable" discharge for having sex with other male marines.

ANNIE LEIBOVITZ

Born 1949, United States

Even if you don't know Annie Leibovitz by name, you know her work. Responsible for some of our most famous photographic portraits, she's snapped everyone from Queen Elizabeth II to RuPaul (see page 38).

While studying painting at the San Francisco Art Institute, Leibovitz found her life's passion through a night class on photography. In 1970, still at university, she took her first professional photos for *Rolling Stone*. Within three years, she was the magazine's chief photographer. In 1980, she took perhaps her most defining photo: John Lennon cuddled naked around Yoko Ono, captured just hours before he was shot dead.

In 1983, she moved to *Vanity Fair*, developing her distinct style of theatrical yet intimate portraits, often inspired by spending hours with her subjects. Her style evolved alongside a relationship with theorist Susan Sontag, who wrote an essay for Leibovitz's photography book *Women*. The two were together until Sontag's death in 2004. Today, Leibovitz continues to work with *Vanity Fair*, as well as *Vogue*.

Leibovitz's career is dotted with landmarks. Most notably, in 1991, she was the first woman to show at the US National Portrait Gallery, and in 2000, was deemed a Living Legend by the Library of Congress.

AND ONE MORE THING ...

Leibovitz doesn't like the term celebrity portraits, instead stating she photographs "people who are good at what they do".

"*You don't have to sort of enhance reality. There is nothing stranger than truth.*"

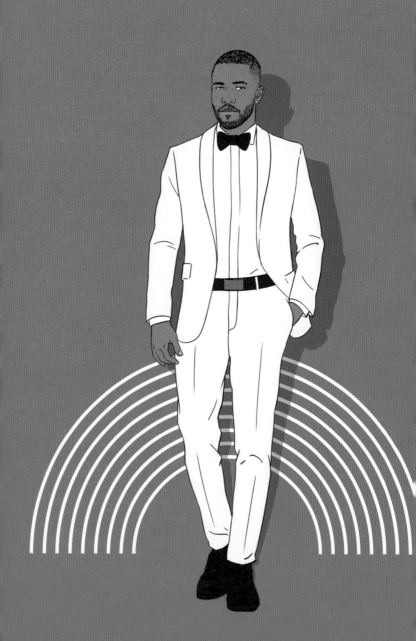

"*There's just some magic in truth and honesty and openness.*"

FRANK OCEAN

Born 1987, United States

Where would music be without Frank Ocean? Not only would it sound completely different, with his avant-R&B production shaping the 2010s, but it would look pretty different, too. It's hard to imagine the plethora of openly queer Black chart-toppers we now have, like Lil Nas X (see page 14), Kevin Abstract, Steve Lacy and Doja Cat, without Ocean.

Starting out as a ghostwriter for the likes of Beyoncé and John Legend, Ocean stepped out with LA hip-hop collective Odd Future (led by fellow queer pioneer Tyler, the Creator) before launching his solo career with a lauded 2011 mixtape, *Nostalgia, Ultra*. In 2012, the week before his debut album *Channel Orange* dropped, he came out via a note on his Tumblr blog – not identifying as any one label, but instead thanking his first love, a man who inspired his wistful album of longing and love lost.

While far from the first openly queer Black rapper (many came before, including Meshell Ndegeocello, Le1f and Big Freedia), Ocean's note and album were a landmark, culture-shifting moment that helped open up a traditionally homophobic genre to queer voices. In 2016, Frank released two albums, *Endless* and *Blonde*, the latter being widely regarded as one of the best releases of the 2010s. An elusive figure, Ocean rarely performs live or makes public appearances – hopefully he's working on his next masterpiece.

AND ONE MORE THING ...

Ocean has a luxury jewellery brand called Homer, which once sold a US$25,570 diamond-encrusted gold cock ring.

CHAZ BONO

Born 1969, United States

Cher has given us so much – seven decades of pop perfection, Bob Mackie looks, *Moonstruck*, tireless AIDS activism, her iconic tweets. Her son, trans advocate Chaz Bono, sits right there among her greatest hits.

Chaz has used his celebrity to bring light to LGBTQIA+ issues, whether working for US gay rights advocate group GLAAD or speaking out against harmful laws. Chaz has also used his personal life to advance LGBTQIA+ rights repeatedly. First, he came out as a lesbian in 1995 on the cover of *The Advocate* and wrote *Family Outing*, a guide for families with LGBTQIA+ members. Then in 2009, he shared that he was a trans man.

Open and honest with the public and press, Chaz endured probing questions and hatred for the sake of education. In 2011, he released both a bestselling memoir *Transition* (his third book) and documentary *Becoming Chaz*, and also competed on *Dancing with the Stars* in the US. In the face of public abuse and death threats, his warmth and bravery won over millions. Undoubtedly, he helped set the ground for what *Time Magazine* in 2014 would call "The Transgender Tipping Point", where the trans rights movement received serious mainstream recognition and attention.

AND ONE MORE THING ...

Bono followed his mum into music with his band Ceremony, releasing just one album, *Hang Out Your Poetry*, in 1993.

"That's what happens when you're finally honest about who you are; you find others like you."

Published in 2024 by Smith Street Books
Naarm (Melbourne) | Australia
smithstreetbooks.com

ISBN: 978-1-9230-4910-9

Smith Street Books respectfully acknowledges the Wurundjeri People of the Kulin Nation, who are the Traditional Owners of the land on which we work, and we pay our respects to their Elders past and present.

Publisher: Hannah Koelmeyer
Editor: Rosanna Dutson
Design: Murray Batten
Illustrations: Phil Constantinesco
Design layout: Heather Menzies, Studio31 Graphics
Project manager: Aisling Coughlan
Proofreader: Pamela Dunne

Printed & bound in China by C&C Offset Printing Co., Ltd.

Book 317
10 9 8 7 6 5 4 3 2 1